Carla Hayden

Librarian of Congress

by Kate Moening

BLASTOFF!
2
READERS

BELLWETHER MEDIA · MINNEAPOLIS, MN

Blastoff! Readers are carefully developed by literacy experts to build reading stamina and move students toward fluency by combining standards-based content with developmentally appropriate text.

Level 1 provides the most support through repetition of high-frequency words, light text, predictable sentence patterns, and strong visual support.

Level 2 offers early readers a bit more challenge through varied sentences, increased text load, and text-supportive special features.

Level 3 advances early-fluent readers toward fluency through increased text load, less reliance on photos, advancing concepts, longer sentences, and more complex special features.

★ **Blastoff! Universe**

Reading Level

Grade **K**

Grades **1–3**

Grade **4**

This edition first published in 2021 by Bellwether Media, Inc.

No part of this publication may be reproduced in whole or in part without written permission of the publisher. For information regarding permission, write to Bellwether Media, Inc., Attention: Permissions Department, 6012 Blue Circle Drive, Minnetonka, MN 55343.

Library of Congress Cataloging-in-Publication Data

Names: Moening, Kate, author.
Title: Carla Hayden : Librarian of Congress / by Kate Moening.
Description: Minneapolis, MN : Bellwether Media, Inc. [2021] | Series: Blastoff! readers: Women leading the way | Includes bibliographical references and index. | Audience: Ages 5-8. | Audience: Grades K-1. | Summary: "Relevant images match informative text in this introduction to Carla Hayden. Intended for students in kindergarten through third grade"– Provided by publisher.
Identifiers: LCCN 2019053737 | ISBN 9781644872086 (library binding) | ISBN 9781681038322 (paperback) | ISBN 9781618919663 (ebook)
Subjects: LCSH: Hayden, Carla Diane, 1952–Juvenile literature. | National librarians–United States–Biography–Juvenile literature.
Classification: LCC Z720.H38 M64 2021 | DDC 027.573092 [B]–dc23
LC record available at https://lccn.loc.gov/2019053737

Editor: Elizabeth Neuenfeldt   Designer: Andrea Schneider

Printed in the United States of America, North Mankato, MN.

Table of Contents

Who Is Carla Hayden?

Carla Hayden is the first African American **Librarian of Congress**.

She is also the first woman to have this job!

a Library of Congress building

Carla grew up in
Tallahassee, Florida.
She loved to read.

Florida

N
W   E
S

Tallahassee

Girl Scouts

Her favorite book was about a black girl in the **Girl Scouts**. Carla was a Girl Scout, too!

Getting Her Start

Chicago
Public Library

Carla moved to Chicago for college. She visited the public library often.

One day, the library was **hiring**. Carla got the job!

Carla Hayden Profile

Birthday: August 10, 1952

Hometown: Tallahassee, Florida

Field: libraries

Schooling:
- studied political science and library science

Influences:
- Colleen Hayden (mother)
- Margaret Pendergast (librarian)

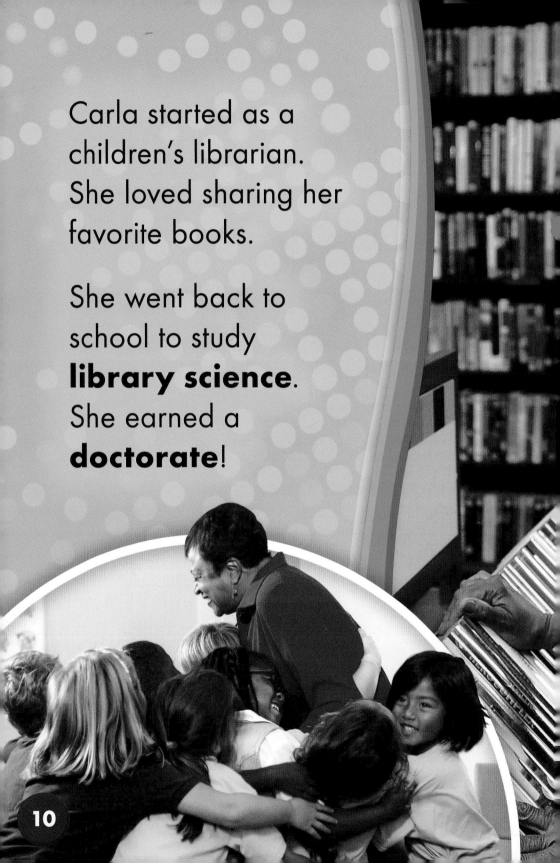

Carla started as a children's librarian. She loved sharing her favorite books.

She went back to school to study **library science**. She earned a **doctorate**!

"CHILDREN NEED TO SEE THEMSELVES... IN BOOKS." (2016)

Changing the World

Carla wanted libraries
to welcome everyone.

She **digitized** many library **collections**. People could easily **access** libraries online!

After **9/11**, the government wanted to see people's library records. But Carla said people should have **privacy**.

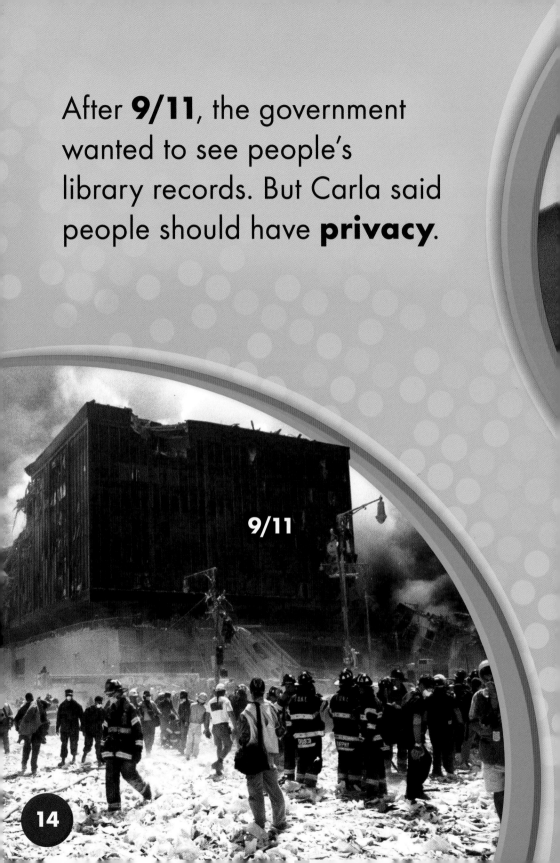

9/11

Some people did not like this.
Carla kept fighting!

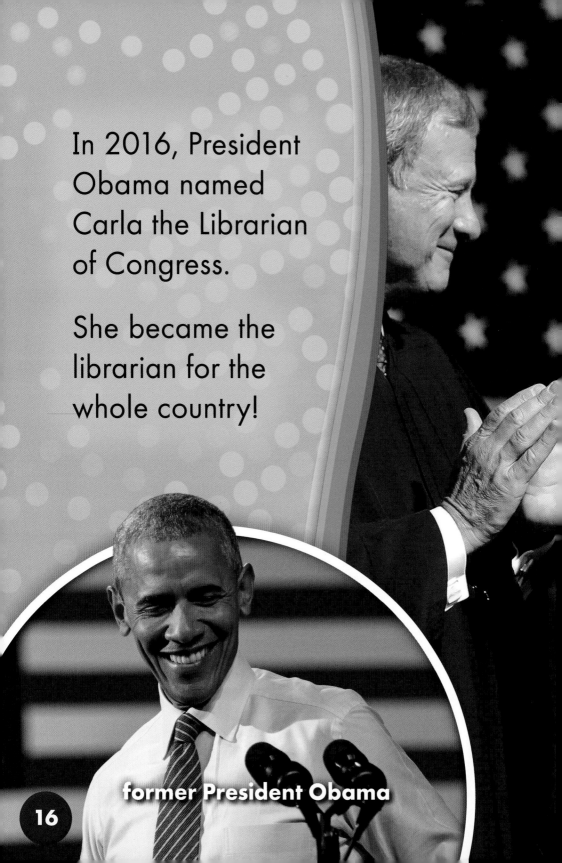

In 2016, President Obama named Carla the Librarian of Congress.

She became the librarian for the whole country!

former President Obama

Carla becoming the Librarian of Congress

"[THE LIBRARY IS] ...A PLACE YOU GET ANSWERS, WHATEVER THE PROBLEM IS." (2018)

Carla's Future

Carla wants to digitize everything in the Library of Congress. In 2018, she digitized more than 7 million items.

This helps people learn from anywhere!

Carla Hayden Timeline

1973 — Carla works her first librarian job with Chicago Public Libraries

1993 — Carla becomes the head of Baltimore's Enoch Pratt Free Library

1995 — Carla is the first African American to be named Librarian of the Year for her work in Baltimore libraries

2003 — Carla is named president of the American Library Association

2016 — Carla becomes Librarian of Congress

Carla is proud
to be the first black
Librarian of Congress.

She wants everyone
to be free to learn.
Libraries help make
this possible!

"I WANT [PEOPLE] TO THINK, YES, IT'S THE LIBRARY OF CONGRESS, BUT IT'S **NOT JUST FOR CONGRESS.**" (2019)

Glossary

9/11—the attack on the United States that happened on September 11, 2001; 9/11 was the biggest attack to ever happen on U.S. soil.

access—to be able to use or get something

collections—groups of things that have been gathered together

digitized—changed into a form that can be accessed on a computer

doctorate—the highest degree that is given by a university

Girl Scouts—a group in the United States for girls to do group activities and learn new skills

hiring—choosing a person for a job

Librarian of Congress—the person who leads the Library of Congress; the Library of Congress is seen as the national library of the United States and is the largest library in the world.

library science—the study of library care

privacy—freedom from public attention

To Learn More

AT THE LIBRARY

Macdonald, Fiona. *You Wouldn't Want to Live Without Libraries!* New York, N.Y.: Franklin Watts, 2018.

Miller, Connie Colwell. *I'll Be a Librarian*. Mankato, Minn.: Amicus, 2019.

Polinsky, Paige V. *Sonia Sotomayor: Supreme Court Justice*. Minneapolis, Minn.: Bellwether Media, 2019.

ON THE WEB

FACTSURFER

Factsurfer.com gives you a safe, fun way to find more information.

1. Go to www.factsurfer.com.

2. Enter "Carla Hayden" into the search box and click 🔍.

3. Select your book cover to see a list of related content.

Index